Printed in the USA
CPSIA information can be obtained
at www.ICGtesting.com
LVHW061832151123
763837LV00085B/71